An Answer to Submission and Decision Making

by
Norman Wright

D1561694

Harvest House Publishers
Irvine, California 92714

AN ANSWER TO SUBMISSION AND
DECISION MAKING
©1977 by Harvest House Publishers,
Irvine, CA 92714
Library of Congress Catalog Card
Number 77-80318
ISBN 0-89081-078-8
All rights reserved. No portion of this book may
be reproduced in any form without the written
permission of the publishers.
Printed in the United States of America.

AN ANSWER TO SUBMISSION AND DECISION MAKING

The biblical directive "Wives, be submissive to your husbands" has recently become a topic of great concern and is often surrounded with confusion. New roles are being suggested for marriage partners. Responsibility for decision making in marriage has also become a focus of debate. Books and articles abound for women, who appear to be more interested in these areas than men and are seeking to discover the application and meaning of the biblical teaching in day-by-day living.

Some suggest that wives should submit to any request of their husband. Others suggest that submission is not taught in the scripture. Still others recommend a form of submission that involves a total submerging of the woman's uniqueness, gifts, and even the repression of honest feelings and thoughts. Some authors offer unique ideas on how to appear submissive on the surface but cleverly suggest manipulative techniques to be used upon one's mate.

Recently a friend of mine went to a Christian bookstore and counted over one hundred books written especially for women (but only nine for men). Most of these books deal with the subject of submission. Many distort biblical teaching and deny the individuality of the woman. Some completely miss the point of the scriptural teaching of HEADSHIP. Most books do not even consider the assignment of roles within the married couple's life nor do they deal specifically enough with the decision-making process. Hopefully, what is presented here will stimulate your thinking on these important issues, whether you are male or female. You may not agree with what is presented, but perhaps you will be challenged to consider what is happening in your own marriage and whether it is (1) biblical and (2) fulfilling your needs and allowing each of you to develop your own unique giftedness.

A marriage relationship should not. be one in which the identity of the wife (or husband) becomes swallowed up in the identity of the other. Rather, it should be an opportunity for each partner to develop fully his or her own special identity. In order to do this, each person needs to be aware of the needs that brought him or her into their marriage relationship.

Ask yourself the following questions. Your answers may clarify what you want, where you are going, and how you are seeking to attain your goals. Writing out your answers will help you to evaluate more carefully your present position.

1. Describe who you are without referring to your job, marital relationship, or family.
2. What needs can you fulfill by yourself?

3. What needs would you like your spouse to help you fulfill?
4. How would you describe your marital relationship at the present time?
5. What would you like it to become?
6. What needs to be done to accomplish this?
7. What is a marital role?
8. What is the role of the wife in marriage?
9. What is the role of the husband in marriage?
10. What five changes would you like to make in yourself to help your marital relationship?
    - (1.)
    - (2.)
    - (3.)
    - (4.)
    - (5.)
11. What five changes would you like your spouse to make to help the marital relationship?
    - (1.)
    - (2.)
    - (3.)
    - (4.)
    - (5.)
12. What does the word *submission* mean to you? To your mate?
13. What personal goal would you like to accomplish in the next five years?
14. What marital goal would you like to accomplish in the next five years?

SUBMISSION

The major question to be considered is "What is submission?" What does it mean? Is it necessary? To help you discover what you believe, a few of the most common questions appear in the following statements. [1] Write your response to them on a separate piece of paper as you may want to ask your spouse to give his answers as well.

1. The scripture teaches that the husband is the head of the family. Therefore, the wife should be submissive and obedient to her husband in everything even if he is an unbeliever.
   a. Agree strongly
   b. Agree with reservations
   c. Disagree strongly
   d. Disagree with reservations

2. Since man is the head of the family, and since this headship is patterned after that of Christ, the husband should be the "boss" of his wife.
   a. Agree strongly
   b. Agree with reservations
   c. Disagree strongly
   d. Disagree with reservations

---

1. H.Norman Wright, *Communication: Key to Your Marriage* (Glendale, Calif.: G/L Publications, Regal Books division, 1974), pp. 22-23, 26.

3. It is alright for the husband to demand obedience or order his wife to respect his authority.
   a. Agree strongly
   b. Agree with reservations
   c. Disagree strongly
   d. Disagree with reservations
4. The husband should make the final decision when he and his wife cannot agree upon a decision that must be made.
   a. Agree strongly
   b. Agree with reservations
   c. Disagree strongly
   d. Disagree with reservations
5. The wife is to be regarded as the one who does the cooking, washing, training of the children, and at the same time she is to be a ''helpmeet'' to her husband.
   a. Agree strongly
   b. Agree with reservations
   c. Disagree strongly
   d. Disagree with reservations
6. It was God's idea that a wife should immediately give up everything to go with her husband.
   a. Agree strongly
   b. Agree with reservations
   c. Disagree strongly
   d. Disagree with reservations

7. It is alright for an obedient wife to instruct and give advice to her husband.
   a. Agree strongly
   b. Agree with reservations
   c. Disagree strongly
   d. Disagree with reservations
8. A wife has the right to disobey her husband when she feels he is dictating to her.
   a. Agree strongly
   b. Agree with reservations
   c. Disagree strongly
   d. Disagree with reservations
9. Since the wife is assigned the subordinate position in marriage, she is not on an equal basis with man.
   a. Agree strongly
   b. Agree with reservations
   c. Disagree strongly
   d. Disagree with reservations

Be subject to one another out of reverence for Christ, the Messiah, the Anointed One. Wives, be subject — be submissive and adapt yourselves — to your own husbands as [a service] to the Lord (Eph. 5:21-22, Amplified).

The word *submit* as used in Ephesians 5:21-22 means the subjection of one individual under or to another. It means to put oneself under the direction of or to arrange oneself under another.

The meaning in this passage is that the wife is to consider obedience that she offers to her husband as obedience offered to Christ. This is not a submission out of fear, a disregard for oneself, nor timidity, but is a submission that is the result of a direct positive decision in the mind of the woman. Gladys Hunt summarized this passage very well in her presentation to the Continental Congress on the Family:

...Submission *is* a biblical idea. God has never liked arrogance or self-centeredness. The teaching of Scripture emphasizes humility as that which pleases God, and Jesus himself spoke of being "meek and lowly of heart." The specific teaching about submission within marriage begins with Ephesians 5:21 where all believers are instructed about relationships, "Be subject to one another out of reverence for Christ." Wives are a specific example of what is required of all Christians; they are to be submissive to their husbands. But the person to whom I submit is my lover, not an enemy, an ogre, or a tyrant. And my lover is to love like Christ. In the end, what is submission but sacrificial self-giving, and what is love but sacrificial self-giving? The wife's submission emphasizes the husband's responsibility as head, but in the end both are demonstrating that Ephesians 5:21 works in relationships because of the new life-style of those who know Jesus Christ.

Personally, biblical authority and my own common sense warn me against wriggling out from under the teaching of the headship of the husband, as if all my freedom and fulfillment depended on being my own head. Paul states that headship is rooted in creation, and as such the husband's authority is given him by God. But how is he to use that authority? The instruction is not, "Be authoritative," but, "Love your wives." The emphasis is on responsibility, and the husband's authority is seen in his enhancing, serving, giving life-style. Both husband and wife are responsible to God, and their responsibilities are two aspects of the same thing. Biblical submission does not spoil quality relationships; our failure is found in the sinfulness that sets us against each other and in our low appropriation of the grace of our Lord Jesus Christ. [2]

Take a moment to write down exactly what the preceding explanation is saying to you. You will have several opportunities to write your own thoughts throughout the remainder of this book, for this exercise will assist you in understanding clearly its message.

2. Gladys Hunt, "A New Look at Christian Wives," *Make More of Your Marriage*, ed. Gary Collins (Waco, Texas: Word Books, 1976), pp. 62-63.

Within the Christian community today, we find many life-styles in which marriage roles of submission and domination vary widely. Bernard Harnik describes some of these life-styles:

1. The husband dominates. The husband rules in all sectors of marriage (or in most of them) and his style is patriarchal. As long as the wife gives in, the marriage will go well, but at the cost of the personal maturing of both partners. With time, disturbances emerge. Frequently the submissive woman will find release elsewhere, tying her children to herself, or developing a friendship hostile to the marriage (or even adulterous), or losing herself in her work. Usually she reacts with opposition to her husband.

2. The wife dominates. The weak husband develops depressions or retreats to extramarital relationships. Sometimes he seeks refuge in alcoholism. I remember a strong and very capable farm wife who revealed her domination even in her outer appearance (she wore trousers and boots). Her husband became a drinker. The more he drank the harder his wife worked. After twenty years of marriage, he ended up in prison having done a number of stupid things while in a drunken stupor. The wife fought for the release of her husband, whom she "loved," in order to "take care of him." Sometimes a henpecked husband will succeed in providing his ruling wife some opposition.

3. Both partners are equally strong and insistent upon their rights. The marriage becomes a constant struggle, marked by more or less heated encounters. Cold and hot wars alternate, interrupted by an occasional armistice. The peace desired in marriage does not come. Nerves and emotions are strained. In old age the power struggle in such a marriage will quiet down, but the marriage will always bear the marks of the struggle.

4. The spouses go their own ways. This is what happens in most marriages when adjustment difficulties are too great, and the result is the mutual alienation of the partners. At the same time, going one's own way can be a weapon against the partner. To the degree that this happens — with money, sex, communication, leisure activities, and so on — the partner is made to feel inferior. It is obvious that such a relationship can end in the disintegration of the marriage and all that it involves.

5. The correct formula can be simply stated: In marriage one may not rule, one serves. If the husband feels stronger, then he must submit himself to his wife's possibilities. If the wife is superior to the husband, she should subordinate herself to him so that he does not lose his dignity. The strong one thus assumes voluntarily the burdens and problems of the weak one. The correct conduct of marriage is always Christian, in

the sense of the biblical admonition, ''Help one another to carry these heavy loads, and in this way you will fulfill the law of Christ'' (Gal. 6:2, NEB). In this sense, the servant formula which Paul recommended to the church in Ephesus (Eph. 5:21 ff.) and in Colossae (Col. 3:18 ff.), and which Peter recommended to the churches (1 Pet. 3:1 ff.), is of eminent importance for the psychohygiene of marriage....[3]

The last life-style described by Harnik offers another key thought concerning the marital relationship. Write down what you feel the author was saying and consider how it applies to your own marital relationship.

Too many Christian wives have encouraged and settled for marital relationships in which the husband is not just the authority but is authoritarian. The final edict in such relationships comes from the male whether he has the ability to decide or not. But the scriptural teaching concerning the role of the husband (which must be understood in order to comprehend the wife's role) is that of servanthood. James Olthuis summarized the relationship:

In the marriage the husband has the office of head. That simply means he has the responsibility and authority to call the marriage — his wife as

3. Bernard Harnik, *Risk and Chance in Marriage* (Waco, Texas: Word Books, 1972), pp. 172-73.

well as himself — to obey the norm of troth. If he faithfully exercises his office, both he and his wife will be freed to be themselves. As the head, the husband is called to take the lead in mutually examining the marriage to see if it is developing according to its long-range goals.

Clearly, headship has nothing to do with being boss. The husband can only command the wife to live up to what the two of them mutually pledged when they married. Likewise, if the husband neglects his office, the wife ought to call the husband back to their mutual vows.

Neither does headship imply inferiority or superiority. Rather, headship is a special office of service so that the marriage may thrive and grow. Headship does not mean that the husband leads or decides in every detail. Once a man and woman have decided which vision of life is going to norm their activities in the marriage, they can leave the decisions in day-to-day affairs to the partner with the appropriate talents, temperaments, and situations. The husband's unique role is to be on guard continually so that the "little" things do not develop into the kinds of patterns that undermine the entire marriage.

...Paul does not say that wives have to be subject to their husbands — period. They are to be subject "as it is fitting in the Lord" (Col. 3:18). The wife's subjection is to the Word of God for marriage; that means being a wife and helping the husband so that the two of them can keep the norm of marriage, the word of troth. That is Paul's concern, one that we often overlook in our zeal to put the husband in a superior position. Only when both husband and wife act as servants, loving and submitting to one another, are marriages pleasing to the Lord. We are subject to the Lord by means of the office he has called us to, whether it be husband or wife. We need to remember that these offices are in marriage and are therefore under the law of troth. Neither the husband nor the wife can demand anything of his partner that is inconsistent with that troth. Neither the husband may lord it over his wife (a perpetual danger), nor the wife over her husband (an imminent danger in Paul's day and often in ours). [4]

As a servant, the husband seeks to fulfill his wife's needs and encourage her to develop her giftedness. In so doing he must allow her to make important decisions on her own. Some husbands don't allow their wife this freedom. Perhaps an example from the field of management would clarify the different styles of leadership.

Douglas McGregor, in his book *The Human Side of Enterprise*, talks about two different types of managers: x-style and y-style. The x-style manager is the authoritarian decision maker. He

4. James H. Olthuis, *I Pledge You My Troth* (New York: Harper & Row, 1975), pp. 27-28.

gives orders to his vice-presidents each morning and watches them do exactly what they were told. This type of manager leaves very little room for the growth, creativity, and development of others except for the times when their ideas parallel his own. The morale and personal development in a company managed by an x-style person is usually quite low. Most individuals do not like to be excluded from the decision-making process or placed in an environment where they cannot grow.

This type of manager also gives orders without asking questions or accepting the suggestions of others. If questioned about his directives, he becomes defensive. His rule is compliance regardless of agreement. He emphasizes a one-person rule and puts others down. His repertoire of orders includes "You do!" and "You must!" He motivates others only by virtue of his position of authority. He often creates an atmosphere of friction, fear, resentment, and hostility.

The y-style manager creates an atmosphere in which others can develop under his leadership. He seeks out their strengths and potential and involves them in areas of responsibility within the company. The communication lines are kept open and he encourages personal growth. This person asks questions and listens to others. He considers alternatives. He respects the freedom and dignity of others and seeks their cooperation. He is not defensive when challenged by others. He leads others and attracts them because of his style. Subordinates may not consider themselves to be in a position of submission because of the freedom and latitude allowed them. If this subordinate position is pointed out to them, they may reply by saying, "Yes! I guess that is so, but I have never thought it a problem because of the way I am growing and because of his leadership style. I want to follow." This leader generates acceptance and cooperation and assists others in relating to one another.[5]

These two styles of leadership can be observed in the husband-wife relationship. The question is not who is in charge in your home, but what is the style of leadership and are Christ's gifts to each individual being cultivated?

Louis Evans, Jr. talked about the healthiness of such a relationship in the book he and his wife coauthored, *My Lover, My Friend*:

The Christian wife submits herself to her husband — of course! My wife submits to me in a hundred different ways! But that is not all. I also submit to her. The Spirit calls us to a mutual submission. "Be subject to *one another* out of reverence for Christ" (Ephesians 5 : 21 RSV) is the key verse here (my italics [Evans']), and *mutual*

5. Douglas McGregor, *The Human Side of Enterprise*, (New York: McGraw-Hill Book Co., 1960).

submission is the overall theme of the verses that follow. A wife is to submit to her husband "as to the Lord" (Ephesians 5:22 RSV) — but that does not mean that her husband *is* her lord. She is to serve her husband in the line of serving Christ. (The Greek word meaning "as" indicates intention, the intention of a wife to serve her husband as he attempts to achieve his dominion over some part of God's creation — just as she serves Christ and the realization of his kingdom.)

Compare Ephesians 5:22 with its parallel passage, Colossians 3:18 RSV: "Wives, be subject to your husbands, as is fitting [proper] in the Lord." This means to us that wives are to please the Lord primarily — and then they are to submit to their husbands as the husbands labor for the Lord's kingdom. A Christian wife will submit whatever resources she has to undergird her husband in his efforts to complete Christ's ministry. She will go with him where he feels God is leading him to work, because he is probably the chief breadwinner. She submits to the valid demands made upon her because of the scheduling involved in his work; she makes the way straight for his endeavors. She is indeed his "helper," someone he needs for his completion, just as he needs the Lord and his resources.

If, however, the husband demands something that is outside the will of Christ and requires the wife to give up those things that belong to Christ or to others, then his wife is under no obligation to obey her husband if in so doing she must disobey Christ, her Lord. Any husband who makes such demands on his wife simply demonstrates his foolishness and misplaced ego.

Some Christian teachers insist that a woman should go along with *anything* her husband asks because he is her "lord." After listening to some of the things such husbands demand of their wives — whether in scheduling priorities or in sexual activities — I am convinced that a wife only reinforces her husband's arrogance and demeans herself by submitting to him. Nobody wins by such appeasement. The wife who goes along with a husband's desire when she feels it is contrary to Christ denies her Lord and permits her husband to stumble headlong into a pit of error.

We understand that many wives during the Watergate debacle were in the dark as to their husbands' activities. But one wife, discovering what her husband was involved in, blew the whistle by calling upon him to act in a moral way. He did! He withdrew from the questionable activities and was not caught in the whirlpool of misdeeds.

I know that if I am bound on a course that Colleen feels will be less than God's best, I am going to hear about it. And I love her for that. If she were to submit to me in such a way as to lessen her clarity of commitment to Christ, I would be very unhappy, because I deeply believe that God's will is the best thing that can happen to us. Often my wife is the instrument of challenge through which I become aware of God's will for my life. I am grateful, even though it may, and sometimes does, sting my male pride. We have seen more marriages blessed because a woman "by her chaste and reverent behavior" was not only loyal to her husband in chastity, but reverent to Christ in obedience, than by a woman covering her Christian witness and denying her Lord.

When the question comes up, "Who's in charge here?" the Christian wife should be able to say, clearly and boldly, "Jesus Christ." [6]

On several occasions my wife Joyce has confronted me about the fact that I had been working too much. The first time that she expressed her feelings about this, I wasn't especially pleased with her comment (even though it *was* phrased properly). The reason I was not pleased was that she was right. On subsequent occasions when she has brought this to my attention I had nearly arrived at the same conclusion, and her comment simply reinforced what I already knew I should do.

6. Louis Evans, Jr., and Colleen Evans, *My Lover, My Friend* (Old Tappan, N.J.: Fleming H. Revell Co., 1976), pp. 39-41.

Neither spouse has all of the wisdom, insights, and spiritual gifts. We need to hear from each other. The husband who resists helpful insights is unfortunately admitting a certain sense of insecurity in his own life which obviously needs improvement. (Here again I am not talking about the woman with an overabundance of opinions who actually calls the shots in the marriage by her dominance evidenced through verbal output.)

An example of how the strengths and abilities of two individuals can be used together happened in our home last year. For Christmas a friend had given me a six-hundred-piece puzzle. I hadn't worked a puzzle for twenty-five years, but Joyce and I set it up on a table in the living room. Gradually, we found ourselves becoming addicted to it, for we couldn't pass through the room without stopping and attempting to put together a few more pieces. Now a puzzle will either teach you patience and endurance or turn you into a raving neurotic! Several times we sat down together and worked on it. It was while we were working together that our different abilities were noticed. Immediately I set out to find all the edge pieces and fit them into place so we would have order and a design to work upon. I noticed that not only was Joyce doing the same, but because of her artistic ability she was sorting the pieces into groups by color and hue. In this way we developed a plan to tackle an enjoyable challenge.

A wife who fails to express her opinions and offer suggestions is not contributing all that she can to the marriage relationship. For a wife to be walked upon like a doormat, she must lie down and allow it to happen. Some wives have asked, "What if my husband says that he doesn't want to hear what I have to say?" A husband controls neither a wife's thoughts nor her freedom to express her opinion! The communication offered ought to follow the proper format and nagging and griping ought to be avoided. But there is nothing wrong with her bringing an issue to the attention of her husband, especially if he has been negligent. [7]

Some wives have asked, "If my husband becomes abusive or even physically violent, should I allow this? Or should I be submissive?" Some have taught that a wife should submit to beatings, but I cannot see that violating one teaching of scripture to fulfill another makes sense. If our bodies are the temple of the Holy Spirit, then we ought not to do anything that would bring harm to the body. That includes allowing one spouse to beat the other. If a husband is allowed to continue this behavior without experiencing any negative

---

7. For a discussion of communication techniques, see *An Answer to Communication* by the same author.

consequences, why should he change? He is simply being allowed to get away with something and in many cases his respect for his wife is lessened.

In a case such as this, a woman ought to calmly let her husband know (when they are not fighting) that if he ever lays another hand upon her, she will either notify the police and sign a complaint against him or separate from him. The shock of informing him of such a plan of action has caused many a husband to seek professional help for this serious problem.

In most marriage relationships, the problems are not this extreme and conflicts are usually over day-to-day matters. In sharing your opinion with your spouse, your attitude, your nonverbal communication, and the tone of your voice are crucial. A wife can still fulfill the scriptural teaching of being submissive and still express herself openly and honestly to her husband. Being supportive does not mean always agreeing with him but rather being free enough to disagree with him and stimulate his own thinking!

Diane and Dick O'Connor, in their book *How to Make Your Man More Sensitive*,[8] have suggested some practical ways for a wife to respond to her husband, which may cause him to behave in

8. Diane and Dick O'Conner, *How to Make Your Man More Sensitive* (New York: E. P. Dutton, 1975).

a more positive manner, and also cause him to take notice of the fact that his wife is a real person. They talked about administering "need shocks" to the husband — a series of actions or statements by the woman, which are different and unexpected but convey the message that the wife is a person with needs and is seeking to fulfill them.

"Need shocks" can be risky because they are different, but by following several important steps a wife can lessen the risk. One suggestion is for the wife to be unassailably reasonable. Men like to think of themselves as the reasonable ones, most feel that they are more rational than women. Men tend to have a stereotyped image of women as beings who are too emotional and therefore do not reason as well as men. A wife who is too emotional would find it helpful to clarify her reasons for her suggestions or for her new style of behavior by writing them down. This is not necessarily a means of proving your point but rather of showing that you have used some creative and logical thinking in the process of coming to your conclusion.

Don't be sidetracked in sharing your reasons. You may find that your spouse is not really interested in listening to your reasons. He may make a comment like, "Oh! That's just a woman's logic." Calmly stick to your point and then ask to hear what he thinks or feels about it. Don't be afraid to ask him for his reasons as well. But what if your husband might become angry, threatened, or defensive, should you still share your opinion? Perhaps it is necessary for a husband to become a bit threatened. He is responsible for his own feelings and he would be better off if he would come to grips with his insecurities and work them through.

Some books being written today have suggested that the woman needs to learn how to "Build the ego of her husband" and to do nothing that would confront or threaten him. It has been said that he needs to be treated with delicacy. Frankly, I think this is ridiculous! Such "ego-building" becomes nothing but a series of manipulative games which are not conducive to an honest relationship. Reinforcing the stereotypes of what a man is and what a woman is (or should be) is not healthy. Honest confrontation and openness may be unnerving and threatening for awhile, but the final prospect of a deeper, more genuine relationship is worth the growing pains.

Most women *are* rational and logical, but men tend to listen to them through a filtering system designed to remove the alleged emotionalism and irrationalism. This pattern of listening communicates to them the message, "You are emotional and illogical." As a result, women are not even given a chance. A woman may use more words to express herself, and deal with an issue with more emotion, and may even use a different form of logic. But that doesn't make her or her beliefs wrong. If you do not win a hearing the first time around, keep trying.

The O'Conners also suggest that you avoid guilty feelings by being reasonable with yourself. Many women feel that they must fulfill the needs of their husband and children first, and then if there is any time and energy left over they can look after themselves. Perhaps by becoming aware of and spending time meeting your own needs, you can be better equipped (and less resentful) to meet your husband's needs. If you say to yourself, "I shouldn't be taking this time for myself," or "If I don't have dinner fixed every night at 5:30 like he wants it, I am a failure," or any other similar statements, challenge their validity. Are they really true?

Another suggestion for building the relationship involves the husband's emotional life. When he responds in a sensitive manner, acknowledge his response and reinforce it. One of the complaints mentioned by women most often is the lack of emotional response they receive from their husband. When he shares his inner concerns and love for you, thank him and let him know that what he has said means a great deal to you. Men in our society are expected to cover and hold in their emotions. They reveal much less about themselves and are more adept at relating impersonally to others. As a result, many married men have remained strangers to their wives.

It is actually for her own benefit that a wife learn to penetrate the outer wall of defense that her husband has erected. Her efforts will not only help the marriage but will also help her husband become more in touch with who he really is. For his physical and emotional health, this help is necessary. A wife should have no qualms about fostering an environment in which her husband can learn to open his life to her (even if he resists the process). Sidney Jourard graphically commented upon this characteristic of men in his book *The Transparent Self*:

It is a fact that suicide, mental illness, and death occur sooner and more often among "men whom nobody knows" (that is, among unmarried men, among "lone wolves") than among men who are loved as individual, known persons, by other individual, known persons. Perhaps loving and being loved enables a man to take his life seriously; it makes his life take on value, not only to himself, but also to his loved ones, thereby adding to its value for him. Moreover, if a man is open to his loved one, it permits two people — he and his loved one — to examine, react to, diagnose, evaluate, and do something constructive about *his* inner experience and his present condition when these fall into the undesirable range. When a man's self is hidden from everybody else, even from a physician, it seems also to become much hidden even from himself, and it permits atrophy — disease and death — to gnaw into his substance without his clear knowledge. Men who are unknown and/or inadequately loved often fall ill, or even die as if suddenly and without warning, and it is a shock and a surprise to everyone who hears about it. One wonders why people express surprise when they themselves fall ill, or when someone else falls ill or dies, apparently suddenly. If one had direct access to the person's real self, one would have had many earlier signals that the present way of life was generating illness. Perhaps, then, the above-noted "inaccessibility" (Rickers-Ovsiankina, 1956) of man, in addition to hampering his insight and empathy, also handicaps him at self-loving, at loving others and at being loved. If love is a factor that promotes life, then handicap at love, a male characteristic, seems to be another lethal aspect of the male role.[9]

It is possible for an overly submissive wife, cooperating with her dominant husband, to assist in promoting the downfall of their relationship even though she believes that she has been faithful in following the scriptural injunction. She has only denied herself and neglected her own growth. James Olthuis describes this process:

9. Sidney Jourard, *The Transparent Self* (Cinncinnati, Ohio: D. Van Nostrant Co., 1964), pp. 30, 52.

When a woman virtually surrenders her personality to her husband, she has less to give to the relationship as the years pass. Outwardly she may seem rather confident, but inwardly she grows more and more dependent until she is only adjunct. Often powerful feelings of hostility well up inside her, against herself for succumbing and against her husband (and God) for demanding such subservience. She feels her marriage is a "trap" with four walls and a husband as keeper.

The situation becomes more complicated when the husband continues to grow through outside contacts while the wife languishes at home. He may have begun to grow away from her when he promised to keep his office problems out of the home. Unfortunately, after years of living separate lives, he may begin to feel that his wife no longer has the understanding to be his confidante and equal. Despite her dutiful obedience and continual adoration, he begins to see her as an embarrassment. Sometimes, feeling guilty, he pampers her even more (just the wrong thing if he wants her to grow-up); at other times he suddenly drops her for "no apparent reason," using her childish behavior (accentuated by his pampering) to justify an affair. [10]

10. Olthuis, p. 36.

A husband can respond if approached openly and honestly. But it will take time. Betty Coble, in her book *Woman: Aware and Choosing*,[11] has suggested some methods of discussion to use with one's husband that may help him to be more open and not feel rejected. A husband will be more open when his wife approaches him and describes what she feels and what she thinks as a contribution of information rather than as a dogmatic pronouncement of a previously determined opinion which she will not change for any reason. He can make better decisions for the family when she contributes information for him to consider.

A wife should also share with her husband what she has learned that has been helpful to her, not just what she thinks he should hear so that he can change. She should not, however, be afraid to suggest to him the changes she would like to see in his life. But she should think through in advance her reasons for sharing this information.

It is also best to compliment him on the things he does right and say little about the areas that are defective. This does not mean the problem areas should not be discussed, but they should not be harped upon. A wife should also remember what the husband *is* contributing to the relationship

11. Betty Coble, *Woman: Aware and Choosing* (Nashville: Broadman Press, 1975).

and let him know that she is aware of this and appreciates his concern and efforts. Understand too that accomplishments mean much to a man and often his attitudes at home are closely related to his work. If he feels successful at work, he feels good as a person. The reverse is also very true. This does not mean that this is the way it ought to be, but a man's work and self-concept are very closely related.

What has been said up to this point? Is submission a valid scriptural principle? Yes it is. but it is a healthy life-giving and fulfilling marital relationship, for the husband's role is one of servanthood. He is to be a servant-leader. Any organization needs one final authority and in the family the husband is it. However, a wise leader, if he knows his strengths and weaknesses, knows when to call upon others who are more qualified than he. In marriage, leadership roles can be worked out through discussion and negotiation based upon the gifts and abilities of each one.

MARRIAGE ROLES

Now, what about the question of roles and responsibilities in marriage? Who does what and why? Does he or she do it? Is it because of tradition or because of what the church has said? Or is it because that is the way it was done in your parent's home?

Failure to clarify the husband-wife roles in a relationship is a major cause of marital disruption. As a couple you are involved in an almost endless number of activities and responsibilities. Each couple should discuss together and decide who is most competent to do which task. Assignment of tasks should not be made simply because of parental example, because it is expected in your social group, or because of tradition. When an individual's abilities, training, and temperament make it difficult or unnecessary to follow an established cultural norm for a role, the couple will need to have the strength to establish their own style of working together. It is imperative that a couple deliberately and mutually develop the rules and guidelines for *their* relationship as husband and wife. This clear assignment of authority and responsibility by the spouses does not create a rigid relationship but allows flexibility and order in what could become a chaotic mess.

Let's spend some time now thinking about your role as a wife or a husband. You will need a good block of time to work through the following questions and evaluation forms. Be sure you write out all of your answers individually before discussing your responses together.

First complete the following sentences and discuss them.

In marriage I believe a "role" is _____

My main role in marriage is _____

I began to form this belief about my role when _____

My mate's role is _____

In marriage a wife should _____

In marriage a husband should _____

I can best help my mate fulfill his or her role by _____

TRADITIONAL MASCULINE ROLES

We all have certain basic ideas of the roles men should play in marriage. List here five basic roles that are usually expected of married men in our society.

1.
2.
3.
4.
5.

Now be creative. Think of four new roles that men might play in marriage — roles that are not usually included in the traditional masculine ideal. They might be roles a man can carry out at home with his children, on the job, or in the community. Try to think of roles that help a man to realize his potential and that contribute to a fuller expression of his personality.

1.

2.

3.

4.

TRADITIONAL FEMININE ROLES

Focus your attention on the traditional feminine roles in marriage. List below five roles that are usually expected of married women in our society.

1.

2.

3.

4.

5.

Next, again be creative. Think of four new roles that women might play in marriage — roles that are not usually included in the traditional feminine ideal. Include new roles in the business world, in the community, in politics, and at home. Try to think of roles that broaden a woman's range of interest and activities and encourage her self-expression.

1.

2.

3.

4.

SHARED ROLES

Great emphasis is being placed on shared role behavior in contemporary marriage. Many of the daily tasks of marriage can be shared by husband and wife. List below four roles that you saw your parents share or that you have observed other couples sharing.

1.
2.
3.
4.

List four roles that you are now sharing in your own marriage.

1.
2.
3.
4.

Use a separate piece of paper for the Role Concepts Comparison that follows. Read each statement and write down the appropriate number indicating what you believe about each one. Then go back and indicate how you think your spouse responded to each statement. Next indicate with a "yes" or a "no" whether *your belief* about the statement is *actually* in practice in your home at the present time. Finally, for each one write down where you obtained your belief — from your parents, pastor, friends, or your own idea.

After each of you has completed the form sit down together and share your responses. Perhaps the husband could start; choosing any statement, read it aloud and then say, "This is how I answered the statement, and this is how I think you answered it." Then the wife can share her responses and you can discuss your answers together.

Remember to consider whether you would like to change any of these beliefs or behaviors. They may be satisfactory or they may not; either way this is your opportunity to discuss them and devise a new plan.

YOUR ROLE CONCEPTS COMPARISON

What do you believe about your role concept in marriage?
Circle:

(1) strongly agree
(2) mildly agree
(3) not sure
(4) mildly disagree
(5) strongly disagree

Wife		Husband
1 2 3 4 5	The husband is the head of the home.	1 2 3 4 5
1 2 3 4 5	The wife should not be employed outside the home.	1 2 3 4 5
1 2 3 4 5	The husband should help regularly with the dishes.	1 2 3 4 5

1 2 3 4 5   The wife has the greater responsibility for the children.   1 2 3 4 5

1 2 3 4 5   Money that the wife earns is her money.   1 2 3 4 5

1 2 3 4 5   The husband should have at least one night a week out with his friends.   1 2 3 4 5

1 2 3 4 5   The wife should always be the one to cook the meals.   1 2 3 4 5

1 2 3 4 5   The husband's responsibility is to his job and the wife's responsibility is to the home and children.   1 2 3 4 5

1 2 3 4 5   Money can best be handled through a joint checking account.   1 2 3 4 5

1 2 3 4 5   Marriage is a 50-50 proposition.   1 2 3 4 5

1 2 3 4 5   Major decisions should be made by the husband in case of an impasse.   1 2 3 4 5

1 2 3 4 5   The husband should babysit one night a week so the wife can get away and do what she wants.   1 2 3 4 5

1 2 3 4 5   A couple should spend their time for recreation and leisure activities with each other.   1 2 3 4 5

1 2 3 4 5	It is all right for the wife to initiate love-making with her husband.	1 2 3 4 5
1 2 3 4 5	The husband and wife should plan the budget and manage money matters together.	1 2 3 4 5
1 2 3 4 5	Neither the husband nor the wife should purchase an item costing more than fifteen dollars without consulting the other.	1 2 3 4 5
1 2 3 4 5	The father is the one responsible for disciplining the children.	1 2 3 4 5
1 2 3 4 5	A wife who has special talent should have a career.	1 2 3 4 5
1 2 3 4 5	It is the wife's responsibility to keep the house neat and clean.	1 2 3 4 5
1 2 3 4 5	Arguments are a definite part of marriage.	1 2 3 4 5
1 2 3 4 5	The husband should take his wife out somewhere twice a month.	1 2 3 4 5
1 2 3 4 5	The wife is just as responsible for the children's discipline as the husband.	1 2 3 4 5
1 2 3 4 5	It is the husband's job to do the yard work.	1 2 3 4 5

1 2 3 4 5		1 2 3 4 5
1 2 3 4 5	The mother should be the one to teach values to the children.	1 2 3 4 5
1 2 3 4 5	Women are more emotional than men.	1 2 3 4 5
1 2 3 4 5	Children should be allowed to help plan family activities.	1 2 3 4 5
1 2 3 4 5	Children develop better in a home with parents who are strict disciplinarians.	1 2 3 4 5
1 2 3 4 5	The wife should always obey what her husband asks her to do.	1 2 3 4 5
1 2 3 4 5	The husband should decide which areas each one should be responsible for.	1 2 3 4 5
1 2 3 4 5	Neither the husband nor the wife should bring their parents into the home to live.	1 2 3 4 5
1 2 3 4 5	Quarrels are always wrong in marriage relationships.	1 2 3 4 5
1 2 3 4 5	It is better to modify the truth to avoid unpleasant situations in the family.	1 2 3 4 5

In the area of roles and responsibilities we can find the concept of spiritual gifts. Louis and Colleen Evans said:

One of the first steps in putting gifts of the Spirit to work in a marriage is to *believe* in such a thesis and to enter into the process of becoming aware, sensitive, and on the lookout for indications of your own and others' gifts.

Not all men are gifted in financial management; sometimes the wives are. In many mature and happy Christian homes we have seen the wife take the initiative in financial matters. True, there was always discussion about the decisions, and in the great majority of the circumstances, there was agreement. But in each, there was a quiet acceptance of her gift and an acquiescence to her counsel even though the "man was the head of the house."

Some men are not gifted in teaching; to require them to be the spiritual teacher as "head of the family" would be to put a heavy burden on their backs as well as create an atmosphere of awkwardness in the process, which repels rather than attracts the student. That does not mean a man might not "teach" in his own style of actions and responses to life's situations.

If the wife's gift is discovered to be something that takes her outside the home, then she and her husband need to consider the place of children in their marriage. If they feel children are right for them, then they ought to set aside the time to do the job right without feeling "hemmed in" or becoming the victims of "cabin fever." The mature woman will not feel pushed out of shape or frustrated in the role of childbearing; she will be able to give herself to this process with joy and delight, for this is a phase of her life. If she cannot raise children in this attitude, then for God's sake and the child's sake she shouldn't have children; no one wants to feel unwanted or that he or she is an inconvenience. But so many, not wanting to "make the sacrifice," are yet pressured by the "standard role" and have children, resisting all the way.[12]

What about a working wife? What about a working mother? These questions stimulate feelings of fear and anger from some. Opinions are varied. Some wives have thoughtfully chosen to be a homemaker and find their fulfillment in that role with no desire for outside employment or for a career. For them, this is a good decision. Other wives have chosen to pursue a career for several years before having children. For them this is right. Yet others have chosen to have an outside job or career and a family at the same time and are successful in both.

I have heard some ministers preach that the only time a Christian wife and mother should be employed is because of economic necessity. It is

---

12. Louis and Colleen Evans, Jr., "Gifts of the Spirit in Marriage," *Make More of Your Marriage*, ed. Gary Collins (Waco, Texas: Word Books, 1976), pp. 38-39.

interesting to note that research indicates that the time when a wife's working is most likely to cause a conflict in the marriage is when her working is due to economic necessity and not the result of her own choice. Latitude is needed in this area of decision making and naturally, even I share a bias which needs to be expressed here. Those who have chosen to be a homemaker and remain at home ought to consider what they will do when the children are grown and on their own. Will there be enough challenge to remain at home or will new areas of endeavor be necessary? Some will need to reach out whereas others will be fulfilled. Karen DeVos, writing in *A Woman's Worth and Work*, says:

In short, whatever the man's headship of the family implies, it does not imply that a woman may not have a career, nor that his career must take precedence over hers, nor that the man must be the sole support of his family, nor that a woman must keep house, nor that she must devote herself to caring for the man's personal needs, nor that all decision making resides in the man.

Christ demands that the church use every ounce of her talent and strength in advancing the kingdom; that she go out dynamically into the world, working and praying mightily; that she develop and grow as much as possible so that there may be greater maturity and ability for the kingdom's work. How many men expect that of their wives?

If a Christian woman can be of service to her God and her fellow humans in a job that her society will not pay for, that career is not of less value than a paid one.

Women should be encouraged to think of their work as a serious commitment to some goal. Their volunteer efforts should not be limited to scattered bits and pieces of help to others, none of which have any real goal or future. Women should be encouraged to take on jobs, whether paid or not, that offer the possibilities for growth, for learning, for developing themselves. They should spend their child-raising years preparing for future responsibilities and leadership opportunities. Christians should never fall victim to the belief that only paid work is worth doing. Neither should they believe that dozens of minor and scattered volunteer efforts will give the satisfaction and growth that a sustained, purposeful effort toward some goal will give. The first chapters of Genesis make very clear that God intended humans to work, not just at easy, quickly accomplished tasks, however necessary, but at difficult, sustained jobs that demand all of one's resources and energy. That kind of work is too seldom asked of women. [13]

13. Karen Helder DeVos, *A Woman's Worth and Work* (Grand Rapids: Baker Book House, 1976), pp. 51, 85.

A child needs the attention of both parents. I feel it is best for the mother to be involved in the rearing of a child during the preschool years rather than leaving the task to a baby-sitter. Later, I believe one of the parents should be at home to meet the child when he arrives after school. But remember that this is my personal bias. Some exceptions to this line of thinking work out quite well. A young couple in our church have been married for several years and have two preschool children. They both teach in a junior high school. The children are left with a young woman during the six to seven hours that the parents are gone during the day. They have quality baby-sitting and both parents have an abundance of time with the children. Neither parent works during Christmas and Easter vacations nor during the entire summer. I don't think that these children will be deprived of a quality relationship with their parents because of the mother working. This mother is a very gifted person and needs both the challenge of home-making and a satisfying career. (Both the husband and wife completed their master's degrees this past year, having attended graduate classes together.)

DECISION MAKING

Who makes the decisions in the marital relationship? Perhaps the question is not who does or who should but who is best qualified. Who in the marital relationship exerts the most influence upon the other or carries more weight in deciding? Some interesting studies have been done on decision making and the balance of power in marriage. Research has shown that the person who contributes more resources to the marriage controls the balance of power. The following facts have been found true of marital relationships.

1. If the male has the dominant personality, he has greater influence. However, even if the wife has the dominant personality, she may not be the most influential member.
2. When the ages of the couple are far apart, the older one exerts more influence.
3. The spouse with the higher educational level has more influence in the marriage than he or she would have otherwise. This sphere of influence is quite noticeable when one mate is college educated.
4. There appears to be confusion concerning the employment status of the wife. It appears that the full-time working wife has the most influence in family decisions but this has not been shown conclusively.

5. The occupational status of the husband has a great deal to do with his status in the home. Most wives recognize that they owe much of their own status to the position of their husbands. Thus they might be dependent upon him even though they are educated. In lower class families in which the wife's income is very essential to the family welfare, the husband's influence is not as great.

6. Children in the home influence the sources of power. Couples who have children appear to be influenced most by the husband, but childless couples are more equalitarian.

7. The stage in the family cycle appears to have some influence. Power in the early marriage relationship is more evenly shared. With the arrival of children the husband seems to dominate, but once the children have left, the pattern shifts to the previous status of more evenly shared power.

Perhaps you have noticed some of these factors in your own marriage; perhaps you have not considered them before.

Every couple directly or indirectly establishes a pattern for reaching marital decisions. Many of these patterns are ineffective or self-defeating. Some bring about lingering feelings of resentment. The majority of couples have not considered how they arrive at decisions. Write your answers to the following questions and then decide how well you have considered the decision-making process.

1. Who makes most of the decisions in your family? How would your spouse answer this question?
2. Have you established guidelines to distinguish between major and minor decisions? If so, what are they?
3. What procedure do you follow when there is an impasse and a decision must be made?
4. How do you decide upon responsibilities for household chores?
5. In what areas of family life do you have the right to make decisions without consulting your spouse? Who decided this policy and how was the decision arrived at?
6. Do you make the decisions that you want to make or the ones that your spouse does not want to make?
7. Do you have any "veto power" over your spouse's decisions? If so, what is the basis for it and how was this decision arrived at?

How did you do in answering these questions? Most couples have never thought them through and yet they are vital to an understanding of the marital relationship.

Here is another way of measuring the influence you exert in your marriage. Here is your opportunity to determine your influence in decision making. Use the following outline, following the instructions and writing your answers on a separate piece of paper. After both of you have done this, exchange papers, compare your answers, and discuss the results together.

Important questions to consider are these: Is each of us making decisions in the areas in which he or she is the most qualified? Does each person have sufficient opportunity to give what he or she has to offer? What is the reason for one or the other having the percentage of influence that is evident?

YOUR PERCENTAGE OF THE DECISION

Describe the decision-making process of your marriage by putting the percentage of influence you have, and the percentage your spouse has, for various issues. The total for each decision must be 100%. (Those who put 50:50 too many times will be considered dishonest.)

	My Vote	Spouse's Vote
Choice of new car.....	_____	_____
Choice of home.....	_____	_____
Choice of furniture....	_____	_____
Choice of your own wardrobe..........	_____	_____

Choice of vacation spots   _____   _____
Choice of decor for the
   home. . . . .   _____   _____
Choice of mutual
   friends. . . . .   _____   _____
Choice of entertain-
   ment. . . . .   _____   _____
Choice of church. . . .   _____   _____
Choice of child rearing
   practices. . . . .   _____   _____
Choice of TV shows. . .   _____   _____
Choice of home menu.   _____   _____
Choice of number of
   children. . . . .   _____   _____
Choice of where we
   live. . . . .   _____   _____
Choice of husband's
   vocation. . . . .   _____   _____
Choice of wife's voca-
   tion. . . . .   _____   _____
Choice of determining
   for what and how the
   money is spent. . . . .   _____   _____

(Place checks by the issues that are not presently
satisfactory to you.)

Consider the following principles and discuss
ways you can implement them in your own marital
relationship concerning the decision-making process.

1. Are the responsibilities and control in the marriage divided on the basis of traditional role expectations or upon what your own parents did? This is a rigid structure in most relationships, but some find definite security within this system. However, when one partner begins to ask "Why do we do it this way?" or when children grow up and leave problems may emerge. The questions arise concerning whether the husband should be the one to wash the car and mow the lawn, and whether the wife should be the one to cook, do the housework, and care for the children. There may be more creative ways of functioning than following the traditional roles.

2. Is the responsibility for making decisions based upon your abilities and giftedness? If so, you probably have a very efficient marriage where each partner can be creative and grow as an individual. In this relationship it is important that each person be aware of what the other is thinking and the direction in which he is growing so they can discuss issues knowledgeably.

3. Does one spouse fail to assume responsibility for making decisions thus forcing the other to make the decision? This has been called decision by default. Usually the one who is affected least by the decision allows the other to make it, and this is not always satisfactory. As

long as one partner takes the abdicated responsibility, he reinforces the apathy of the other. It might be best not to take the responsibility so readily but to discuss the matter fully. Too many husbands turn the responsibility for child rearing decisions over to their wives, but the scripture indicates that the father is to be involved with the child. Note the following verses describing the father's task:

To rule — 1 Timothy 3:12,3,4

To chasten — Proverbs 19:18

To correct — Proverbs 22:15; 23:13

To teach — Deuteronomy 6:7; 11:18-21; Proverbs 1:8; 4:1-4

To nurture — Ephesians 6:4

Not to provoke to anger — Colossians 3:21

To provide for — 1 Timothy 5:8; 2 Corinthians 12:14

To encourage — 1 Thessalonians 2:11

To command — Genesis 18:19

To guide — Jeremiah 3:4

To discipline — Proverbs 3:12; Hebrews 12:5-7

4. Do you discuss together your methods for decisions? If not, sit down together during a time when no major decision must be made and work out the process that you will follow.

5. If you and your spouse are using a set method of making decisions and it is not working well,

experiment with another. Develop several different approaches.

6. Have you ever asked your spouse if he has difficulty making decisions? Is it easy for him? Does he know whether it is difficult for you or easy for you? You cannot always judge by his outward behavior. He may be experiencing some inner conflict and may welcome input from you.

7. Have you agreed to make decisions in certain areas on your own without interference from your spouse? Many couples have numerous areas in which one is responsible for making decisions on his own. Some couples put a dollar limit on household or hobby items and do not have to consult the other unless the price exceeds the limit. One man stated in one of our seminars that in the last ten years he had not purchased one new item of clothing for himself. His wife buys everything and he is very satisfied with this arrangement. He hates to shop and he trusts her judgment. One couple stated that when they purchase a car that she will drive, she is primarily responsible for the choice and when it is for him, he has more to say.

8. What are some of the major decisions that each of you makes? What are the minor ones? How do you feel about these? Is there an area in which you would like some assistance from your

spouse or one in which you would like a greater voice? Some couples have written job division lists and then considered who has the time, ability, and expertise to get each job done. They consider who is more concerned with each area and who enjoys the task the most.[14]

Finally, it's essential to realize that the spouse who *makes* the decisions is not necessarily the spouse who *controls* them. The key question ultimately is, "Who *decides* who decides?"

Husbands or wives often "delegate" decision areas to their partners so that while the actual decision is made by one, there is no doubt that the other holds the power. As we have pointed out, sometimes the "weaker" partner may actually have his or her mate jumping through hoops. A "helpless" husband may ask his wife to lay out his clothing every morning so that his socks, shoes, tie, shirt, and suit will coordinate. *She decides* what he will wear, but *he has decided* that she is to be his "valet." A "depressed" wife may have everyone in the household catering to her "bad" days. Many books and articles have been written telling wives how to fool husbands into believing they are "lords and masters" by appearing to defer to them on the surface. This game playing backfires in the long run. Finding the patterns you

14. Adapted from Marcia Laswell and Norman M. Lobsenz, *No Fault Marriage: The New Technique of Self-Counseling and What It Can Help You Do*, (Garden City, N.Y.: Doubleday & Co., 1976).

use to make decisions, altering them to suit your needs, and having a variety of decision-making methods to use for different circumstances are the realistic and effective techniques that make a marriage function well.[15]

One of the major questions usually asked has to do with the impasse. When each person is committed to his own point of view or belief, further negotiation seems unlikely to produce any change.

James Jauncey, in his book *Magic in Marriage*, points out that the Christian husband and wife have specific help for everyday problems, not only from the guidelines in scripture, but also in the daily presence of the Holy Spirit. Jauncey says:

God through His Holy Spirit seeks our best welfare and happiness. He seldom does this by a supernatural act. Instead, He seeks to permeate our thinking until our judgments are His.

In marriage He has two people to work through. The husband's authority does not carry infallibility with it. Since the two have become "one flesh" the guidance has to come through both. This means that except in cases of emergency, decisions affecting the whole family should not be put into effect until they are unanimous.[16]

15. Laswell and Lobsenz, p. 201.
16. James Jauncey, *Magic in Marriage* (Waco, Texas: Word Books, 1968), pp. 126-27.

This view is also held by Lionel Whiston. In his book *Are You Fun to Live With?* he says:

By far the most productive and ideal method of dealing with decisions is to make them together under God. This rules out the possibility of taking over areas of responsibility in open defiance, in secret, by emotional blackmail, or by constantly placating the offended partner.

The prelude to making joint decisions under God is the commitment of the partners to Him, as individuals and as a team. It relies on wisdom and direction greater than that of either partner, claimed by faith. Practically, it means examining all the factors involved, "putting the cards on the table," including pertinent data, inner motives and desires, the recognition of which spouse has greater experience in the particular area, and lessons learned in the past.[17]

This view presupposes that both individuals are honestly seeking the will of God for their lives and are completely willing to follow the will of God. Many times a husband and wife will decide that it is better for one or the other to make decisions in different areas of responsibility. Many a wise husband, realizing the capabilities and strengths of his wife, has delegated definite responsibilities and authority where the wife can best comple-

17. Lionel Whiston, *Are You Fun to Live With?* (Grand Rapids: Zondervan Publishing House, 1960), pp. 110-11.

ment him. Each relies upon the strength and wisdom of the other person. What happens when the husband and wife cannot agree upon a decision that must be made? In cases like this perhaps the husband should decide. This does not mean it will be the best decision, but God will hold the man responsible for the decision, not the woman.

A final challenge and summary is best stated by Gladys Hunt:

That two persons could be open with each other, sharing deeply, transparent in the most intimate areas of life, forgiving each other, serving each other, transcending self to enhance and affirm each other — this quality relationship needs to be openly declared as that larger good that we seek in Christian marriage. This kind of beauty, this kind of fulfillment of our humanity makes a worthy goal for Christian wives. Nothing less will do.

This is also what makes home a safe place, not two people standing over against each other, trying to manipulate the other to please self, but two people standing beside each other and sharing life openly. Their embracing relationship is a fragrance of life, of faithfulness, of truth in a world of suspicion and anxiety. These two are not perfect, but they are a growing, loving, redeeming society, and what they are becoming is seen again in their children. Together they make a safe place in a fractured, cold world where others are warmed and encouraged by their love.

This is not some high-minded dream that lacks reality; it is coming to grips with the reality of redemption. When women have won all their rights and honor and equal opportunity we will still face our emptiness if we have not worked out our human relationships. After we have tried all the new fads of practical manifestations of submissiveness, we will still have to face the needs of our own personhood and a deep urgency to experience quality oneness with another person. This is our basic need; its potential is found in the cross.

I would issue a new call to an old truth — a new call to Christian wives to maintain, to insist upon, to establish quality relationships in our lonely alienated world and to be satisfied with nothing less. We are recalled to our human potential, redeemed by God's grace. [18]

18. Hunt, pp. 54-55.